The One
Leader Guide

The One:
Reaching the Lost
with the Love of Christ

Participant Book
978-1-7910-0031-8
978-1-7910-0032-5 *ePub*

Leader Guide
978-1-7910-0033-2
978-17910-0034-9 *ePub*

DVD
978-1-7910-0035-6

LEADER GUIDE

A Bible Study from Luke 15

the o1ne

reaching the lost with the love of Christ

Jim and Jennifer Cowart

JENNY YOUNGMAN, CONTRIBUTOR

Abingdon Press | Nashville

THE ONE
REACHING THE LOST WITH THE LOVE OF CHRIST
LEADER GUIDE

Copyright © 2021 Abingdon Press
All rights reserved.

No part of this work may be reproduced or transmitted in any form or by any means, electronic or mechanical, including photocopying and recording, or by any information storage or retrieval system, except as may be expressly permitted by the 1976 Copyright Act or in writing from the publisher. Requests for permission can be addressed to Permissions, The United Methodist Publishing House, 2222 Rosa L. Parks Blvd., Nashville, TN 37228-1306 or e-mailed to permissions@umpublishing.org.

ISBN 978-1-7910-0033-2

Unless otherwise indicated, scripture quotations are taken from the Holy Bible, New Living Translation, copyright ©1996, 2004, 2015 by Tyndale House Foundation. Used by permission of Tyndale House Publishers, Inc., Carol Stream, Illinois 60188. All rights reserved.

Scripture quotations marked (ESV) are from the ESV Bible (The Holy Bible, English Standard Version®), copyright © 2001 by Crossway, a publishing ministry of Good News Publishers. Used by permission. All rights reserved.

Scripture quotations marked MSG are taken from THE MESSAGE, copyright © 1993, 1994, 1995, 1996, 2000, 2001, 2002 by Eugene H. Peterson. Used by permission of NavPress. All rights reserved. Represented by Tyndale House Publishers, Inc.

Scripture quotations marked (NIV) are taken from the Holy Bible, New International Version®, NIV®. Copyright © 1973, 1978, 1984, 2011 by Biblica, Inc.™ Used by permission of Zondervan. All rights reserved worldwide. www.zondervan.com The "NIV" and "New International Version" are trademarks registered in the United States Patent and Trademark Office by Biblica, Inc.™

Scripture quotations marked NKJV are taken from the New King James Version®. Copyright © 1982 by Thomas Nelson. Used by permission. All rights reserved.

21 22 23 24 25 26 27 28 29—10 9 8 7 6 5 4 3 2 1
MANUFACTURED IN THE UNITED STATES OF AMERICA

CONTENTS

About the Authors 7
Introduction 9
Small Group Leader Helps 15
The Three Parables of Luke 15 18

Small Group Session Outlines 23
Session 1: You Are the One 25
Session 2: The Sheep 33
Session 3: The Coin 41
Session 4: The Boys 49

Resources for a Church-wide Emphasis 57
Reaching the One: Overcoming Obstacles 59
Planning a Church-wide Emphasis 67
Weekly Memory Verses 77
Weekly Sermon Starters 79

A Final Word of Encouragement 91

ABOUT THE AUTHORS

Jim Cowart is the lead and founding pastor of Harvest Church in Middle Georgia, a congregation that he and his wife, Jennifer, began in 2001 and that has twice been named among the nation's fastest-growing congregations. Jim has authored and coauthored numerous books including *Leading from Horseback*; *Grab, Gather, Grow*; and *Start This, Stop That*. Whenever life allows, Jim escapes to enjoy the outdoors on horseback, hunting, and traveling with his family.

Jennifer Cowart is executive and teaching pastor of Harvest Church. With degrees in Christian education, counseling, and business, she has been integral to the development of the Emerging and Discipleship Ministries at Harvest, which include more than three hundred small groups that meet in homes and workplaces. She is the author of two women's Bible studies (*Fierce* and *Messy People*) and several small group studies coauthored with her husband, Jim, including *Hand Me Downs* and *Living the Five*. Jen is an avid moviegoer and travel enthusiast. She and Jim love doing life with their kids, Aly, Josh, and Andrew.

INTRODUCTION

The Story of *The One* and Our Hope for You

We have always been passionate about reaching people for Christ. Evangelism is at the core of who we are and how we do ministry. Since beginning Harvest Church in 2001, we have had the privilege of seeing more than four thousand people accept Jesus as their Savior. We have tried to be very intentional in creating a culture that welcomes those far from God. But when we took a hard look at the question "Who is your One?" we found that we were no longer as intentional as a church family and as individuals as we had been at one time. The balance was off. We didn't mean to drift, but we had. Without realizing it, we had become so occupied with the care and discipleship of all of these believers that we were neglecting the work of reaching out to those in our community who had not yet found God relevant in their lives—the lost. As a body of believers, we had to wrestle with how to put Luke 15 and the Great Commission into practice in new and fresh ways.

So, our team got to work dreaming new dreams and reintroducing a culture of invitation and passion for the lost in our local setting. Through a four-week series of sermons and small group sessions on the three parables in Luke 15, we cast a vision and invited people to look for new and creative ways to reach those in their lives who did not have a relationship with Jesus. And, if we are honest, we wondered if our people even knew people who were living far from God. *Maybe we had already reached the people in our lives who aren't Christ-followers*, we thought. *Maybe our church members don't really know many lost people.*

We quickly discovered that these concerns were unfounded.

During our four-week emphasis, called *The One*, we asked our people to write on the back of simple cards the first names of people in their lives who did not have a relationship with Jesus. In other words, we asked them to identify their One, or Ones. Then, at the end of each service, people were invited to come forward and pin their cards to a display on the altar. We told them that we would pray for their Ones to have open hearts, and for them to have the courage to reach out and invite them to church. We did this all four weeks of the series. Those cards stayed up the entire series, and the staff faithfully prayed over the cards (not card by card, but overall). At the end of the month as we took the cards off the altar, we looked more carefully at what was on them.

Two things surprised us. First, there were over forty-two hundred names listed! Wow! We had not lost touch with those living far from God. We had just stopped doing much about it.

Our second surprise was that many of the cards simply said "Me." When they were allowed to be anonymous and vulnerable, many of those attending services admitted that *they* were the lost sheep, the lost coin, and the lost boy(s).

Our work was not done—and our neither is yours.

In order to kick-start our renewed emphasis on welcoming the community into the doors of the church, we also began new ministries—outreach initiatives designed specifically to reach the unchurched in our area. One of those ministries was to sponsor several community-wide free Friday Night Block Parties. (Note: The word *free* matters to people!) Live music, activities for kids, food trucks, and seasonal attractions were offered, and in six months we had over twelve thousand people participate. This got people onto the church property and comfortable with our setting. Almost immediately we saw our first-time worship attendance skyrocket, and this gave us the privilege of sharing Christ with new people. Best of all, we began to see more and more people accepting Christ.

It has been over a year since our church did this series, but only last week a man met us in the lobby and said, "Hey, it has taken a while, but I think my One will be here today. So...don't blow it today, OK?" Our friend had been praying for his friend for a year, hoping that somehow his One would come to know and love God. This man was invested, and he wanted to be sure we were on the job that day! (Like most pastors, we try not to ever blow it when we're speaking, but knowing that the One is sitting out there does keep us on our toes!)

About This Study

Before the first session, you will want to distribute copies of the participant book to the members of your group. Be sure to communicate that they are to read the first chapter before your first group session.

As you gather each week with your group, you will have the opportunity to watch a video, discuss and respond to what you're learning, and pray together. You will need access to a television and DVD player with working remotes.

This leader guide and the DVD will be your primary tools for leading each group session. In this book you will find outlines for four group sessions, each formatted for a 60-minute session:

    Leader Prep (Before the Session)
Gathering	3 minutes
Warm Up	5 minutes
Memory Verse	1 minute
Video	10-12 minutes
Group Discussion	30-35 minutes
Call to Action and Prayer	3-5 minutes

Feel free to adapt or modify the format in any way to meet the specific needs and preferences of your group. If you would like to extend the session to 90 minutes, simply increase the group discussion and prayer time. Here is a brief overview of the elements included.

Leader Prep (Before the Session)

This section provides an overview of the week's Scriptures and themes, a recap of the corresponding chapter, a list of materials and equipment needed, and some session goals. Be sure to read this section, as well as the session outline, before the session. You also may find it helpful to review the DVD segment in advance.

Gathering (3 minutes)

You may find that participants are rushed and distracted as they arrive (yourself included). Invite the group to settle in and open their hearts to what God might have for them during your time together. You may choose to read the written prayer provided for you or to pray an opening prayer of your own.

Warm Up (5 minutes)

Each session includes a brief warm-up exercise to introduce the topic and set the tone for discussion.

Memory Verse (1 minute)

Each week you'll recite together the memory verse from that week's chapter.

Video (10-12 minutes)

Next, watch the week's video segment together.

Group Discussion (30-35 minutes)

After watching the video, use the discussion points and questions provided to facilitate group discussion. The discussion points are excerpts from the corresponding chapter of *The One*. You may choose to read aloud the discussion points or express them in your own words. Use one or more of the questions that follow to guide your conversation.

We have provided more discussion questions than you will have time to include. Beforehand, select those you want to cover, and put a check mark beside them. Reflect on each question and make some notes in the margins to share during your discussion time.

Rather than attempting to bulldoze through, be open to where the Spirit takes the conversation. Remember that your role is not to have all of the answers but to encourage discussion and sharing.

Call to Action and Prayer (3-5 minutes)

Invite participants to put what they have learned into practice by engaging in prayer practices that call to mind people in their lives who might be lost or far from God.

Then close by leading the group in prayer. Invite the group to name prayer requests. You might share a request of your own to get things started. Encourage members to participate in the closing prayer by praying aloud for one another and the requests given. Make sure name tags are visible so that group members do not feel awkward if they do not remember someone's name. After the prayer, remind the group to pray for one another and their Ones throughout the week.

Before You Begin

As group leader, your role is to guide and encourage the group to fully participate in the group experience. Wherever they are in their faith journey, invite them to seek God, open their hearts, and be responsive to the Holy Spirit, expecting an encounter with our loving God who searches for lost things.

SMALL GROUP LEADER HELPS

- Pray for wisdom and discernment from the Holy Spirit, for you and for each member of the group, as you prepare for the study.
- Before each session, familiarize yourself with the content. Read the designated book chapters and read through the session outline in this leader guide. You also may want to view the video in advance.
- Choose the session elements you will use during the group session, including the specific discussion questions you plan to cover. Be prepared, however, to adjust the session as group members interact and as questions arise. Prepare carefully, but also allow space for the Holy Spirit to move in and through the group members and through you as facilitator.
- Prepare the space where the group will meet so that the space will enhance the learning process. Ideally, group members should be seated around a table or in a circle so that all can see

one another. Movable chairs are best, so that the group can easily form pairs or small groups for discussion.
- Create a climate of openness where participants feel encouraged to contribute to the discussion. Remember that some people will jump right in with answers and ideas, while others will need time to process what is being discussed.
- If you notice that some participants seem never to be able to enter the conversation, ask them if they have thoughts to share. Give everyone a chance to talk, but keep the conversation moving. Moderate to prevent the same few individuals from doing all the talking.
- Do not be afraid of silence. If no one speaks in response to a question, count silently to ten, then say something such as, "Would anyone like to go first?" If no one responds, offer an answer yourself and ask for comments.
- Model openness as you share with the group. Group members will follow your example. If you limit your sharing to a surface level, others will follow suit.
- Encourage multiple answers or responses before moving on.
- Ask "Why?" or "Why do you believe that?" or "Can you say more about that?" to help facilitate the discussion and give it greater depth.
- Affirm others' responses with comments such as "Great" or "Thanks" or "Good insight"—especially if it's the first time someone has spoken during the group session.

- Monitor your own contributions. If you are doing most of the talking, back off so that you do not train the group to listen rather than speak.
- Remember that you do not have all the answers. Your job is to keep the discussion going and encourage participation.
- Honor the schedule. If a session is running longer than expected, get consensus from the group before continuing beyond the agreed-upon ending time.
- Involve group members in various aspects of the group session, such as saying prayers or reading the Scripture.
- Note that the session guides sometimes call for breaking into smaller groups or pairs. This gives everyone a chance to speak and participate fully. Mix up the groups; don't let the same people group up for every activity.
- As always, in discussions that may involve sharing personal information, confidentiality is essential. Participants should never pass along stories that have been shared in the group. Remind participants at each session that confidentiality is crucial to the success of this study.

THE THREE PARABLES OF LUKE 15

Parable of the Lost Sheep

⁴"If a man has a hundred sheep and one of them gets lost, what will he do? Won't he leave the ninety-nine others in the wilderness and go to search for the one that is lost until he finds it? ⁵And when he has found it, he will joyfully carry it home on his shoulders. ⁶When he arrives, he will call together his friends and neighbors, saying, 'Rejoice with me because I have found my lost sheep.' ⁷In the same way, there is more joy in heaven over one lost sinner who repents and returns to God than over ninety-nine others who are righteous and haven't strayed away!"

(Luke 15:4-7)

Parable of the Lost Coin

⁸"Or suppose a woman has ten silver coins and loses one. Won't she light a lamp and sweep the entire house and search carefully until she finds it? ⁹And when she finds it, she will call in her friends and neighbors and say, 'Rejoice with me because I have found my lost coin.' ¹⁰In the same way, there is joy in the presence of God's angels when even one sinner repents."

(Luke 15:8-10)

Parable of the Lost Son

¹¹To illustrate the point further, Jesus told them this story: "A man had two sons. ¹²The younger son told his father, 'I want my share of your estate now before you die.' So his father agreed to divide his wealth between his sons.

¹³"A few days later this younger son packed all his belongings and moved to a distant land, and there he wasted all his money in wild living. ¹⁴About the time his money ran out, a great famine swept over the land, and he began to starve. ¹⁵He persuaded a local farmer to hire him, and the man sent him into his fields to feed the pigs. ¹⁶The young man became so hungry that even the pods he was feeding the pigs looked good to him. But no one gave him anything.

¹⁷"When he finally came to his senses, he said to himself, 'At home even the hired servants have food enough to spare, and here I am dying of hunger! ¹⁸I will go home to my father and say, "Father, I have sinned against both heaven and you, ¹⁹and I am no longer worthy of being called your son. Please take me on as a hired servant."'

²⁰"So he returned home to his father. And while he was still a long way off, his father saw him coming. Filled with love and compassion, he ran to his son, embraced him, and kissed him. ²¹His son said to him, 'Father, I have sinned against both heaven and you, and I am no longer worthy of being called your son.'

²²"But his father said to the servants, 'Quick! Bring the finest robe in the house and put it on him. Get a ring for his finger and sandals for his feet. ²³And kill the calf we have been fattening. We must celebrate with a feast, ²⁴for this son of mine was dead and has now returned to life. He was lost, but now he is found.' So the party began.

²⁵"Meanwhile, the older son was in the fields working. When he returned home, he heard music and dancing in the house, ²⁶and he asked one of the servants what was going on. ²⁷'Your brother is back,' he was told, 'and your father has killed the fattened calf. We are celebrating because of his safe return.'

²⁸"The older brother was angry and wouldn't go in. His father came out and begged him, ²⁹but he replied, 'All these years I've slaved for you and never once refused to do a single thing you told me to. And in all that time you never gave me even one young goat for a feast with my friends. ³⁰Yet when this son of yours comes back after squandering your money on prostitutes, you celebrate by killing the fattened calf!'

³¹"His father said to him, 'Look, dear son, you have always stayed by me, and everything I have is yours. ³²We had to celebrate this happy day. For your brother was dead and has come back to life! He was lost, but now he is found!'"

(Luke 15:11-32)

Small Group Session Outlines

YOU ARE THE ONE

ONE

Leader Prep

Session Goals

Through this session's discussion participants will:

- explore the story of Zacchaeus,
- see themselves as the one whom Jesus chooses, and
- be invited to pray for someone they know who needs to experience being chosen by God.

Preparation

- Read the first chapter, "You Are the One," in *The One* by Jim and Jennifer Cowart.
- Read through this session outline in its entirety to familiarize yourself with the material being covered.
- Read and reflect on the following Scriptures: Luke 15:7, 9, 20; 19:1-10; John 3:16.
- Have a markerboard or large sheet of paper available for recording group members' ideas.

- Have a Bible, paper for taking notes, and a pen or pencil available for every participant.

What You Will Need

- *The One* DVD and DVD player
- Stick-on name tags and markers (if needed)
- Slips of paper and pens
- Extra Bibles

Session Outline

Gathering (3 minutes)

If group members do not know one another well, hand out name tags and markers and ask participants to write their names on the name tags and wear them for the session. Welcome the participants and remind them that you will be spending the next four weeks exploring what it means to reach the lost with the love of Christ and how we as believers can do this. When you are ready to begin the session, pray the opening prayer below or a prayer of your own.

Lord, thank you for choosing us, for chasing after us, and for calling us your very own. Thank you for your presence as we study what it means to be the One; in Jesus's name. Amen.

Warm Up (5 minutes)

- When have you lost something and torn your house apart trying to find it? Explain.
- Have you heard the phrase, "You'd lose your head if it wasn't attached"? Would you say that describes you? Why or why not?

Memory Verse (1 minute)

Say aloud together the memory verse for Week 1:

"Believe in the Lord Jesus, and you will be saved."
(Acts 16:31 NIV)

Video (10-12 minutes)

Play the Week 1 video segment on the DVD.

Group Discussion (30-35 minutes)

Video Discussion

- How would you describe the culture in your church as it pertains to reaching out to lost people?
- In the story of Jill and her son Drew, Jill said, "When you're really searching for something, pride can't determine what you do." How do you think pride keeps us from reaching out to those who are lost or far from God?
- In the video, Jim said, "You are the One…you are the object of great worth." Why do you think understanding how much God loves you is so important as we talk about inviting those who are lost or far from God to church?

Book Discussion

More discussion points and questions have been provided than you will have time to include. Beforehand, select those you want to cover, and place a check mark beside them. Page numbers from the book are provided for reference.

1. "Imagine the setting, the city of Jericho. It's hot. The hills beyond the palms are barren, but there is life in town because the teacher everyone has been talking about is coming through. Jesus, the healer, the controversial leader, has come to town, and the crowds have gathered. Now, put yourself into the

story, imagining that you are Zacchaeus. You want to get to Jesus. But, like at a political rally or concert, the crowd is a dense mass of humanity, and getting a front-row seat seems impossible. So, you have a crazy idea: I'll climb this tree and get a balcony seat for the show." (pages 3-4)

- Read Luke 19:1-10. What did you feel as you heard the story? Could you relate to Zacchaeus? Explain. What did you feel as you were singled out in the crowd and then allowed to host Jesus in your home?
- What did you feel as you realized that Jesus knows your name, and he called to you today?
- When are times you've felt like Jesus might be calling to you? What were those experiences like?

2. "Zacchaeus had hurt many people. He had done things he was not proud of and surely stood in need of forgiveness from many. He was a sinner living far from God. But Jesus called his name. Zacchaeus did not deserve the attention and grace shown to him. But, then again, neither do we. It's easy to imagine the outrage of the crowd, but what was Zacchaeus feeling? Could he even imagine that someone so pure, so loving, would want to spend time with him? Now, remember that…you are the One in the tree. Jesus is calling your name." (page 5)

- What reactions would you expect from the people as they watched Jesus invite Zacchaeus into relationship?
- What reactions do you imagine Zacchaeus had as the crowd demonstrated its disapproval?

What about his reactions as Jesus called him down from the tree?
- What do you think Jesus was teaching the crowd—and us—about the love of God?

3. "Before we become passionate about sharing Christ with others, we have to become secure in the fact that he first loved us. We have to personalize his promises and come to a heartfelt understanding that we are God's dearly loved children." (page 6)
    - Read Romans 5:8. How would you paraphrase this verse in your own words?
    - What does this verse mean about God's love for us?
    - Would you say it's easy or difficult for you to believe that God loves you (and always has)? Explain.

4. "For God so loved the world that he gave his one and only Son" (John 3:16 NIV). OK, I understand that. For God so loved Jim, and my kids, and my staff—of course, *they're* all precious. Surely this applies to them"—but not to me. (page 6)
    - Have you ever struggled to believe that you are *precious* to God? Explain.
    - Why is it so easy to imagine God's depth of love for others and to forget that this same depth of love is available to us?
    - Was there a time in your walk with God when you struggled to believe God's love and mercy applied to you? If you're comfortable, share about that time.

5. "One of our dear friends is a Maasai warrior in Kenya. He is also a precious man of God. When we see him, he often greets us with the traditional African greeting of *'I see you.'* ... It is a verbal declaration of more than acute eyesight. It is his warm way of saying, *I know you, I care about you, I love you.* Likewise, when Jesus calls to Zacchaeus, he is saying, 'I see you. I value you. Let's spend time together. You are important.'" (page 6)

   - Why do you think it is so important for us to feel seen and known?
   - How do you communicate "I know you, I care about you, I love you" to your loved ones?
   - What might our communities—or even the world—look like if we really saw and loved one another? How might they be different if we really believed that Jesus knows us, cares about us, and wants to spend time with us?

6. "Jesus welcomed messy people. Tax collectors like Zacchaeus, along with other notorious sinners like me and probably like you, often spent time listening to Jesus share life-giving truths." (page 7)

   - Has it ever bothered you that Jesus welcomed messy people into his fold? Why or why not?
   - Would you consider yourself "messy"? Why or why not?
   - Why do you think Jesus had so many encounters with messy people throughout the Gospels?

7. "A meal during this time period was not fast-food pickup. It was a social event, usually hours long. So, when the Scripture mentions that Jesus took the time to eat with these people who were not

considered holy by the Pharisees' standards, he was spending quality time with them. He cared about their stories. Jesus wanted to know them, and he wanted them to know him. He didn't just allow them to listen in as he instructed the more righteous members of the community. They weren't his pet projects. He spent time with them and considered them friends." (page 7)

- When was the last time you had a significant gathering around a meal? Who was there? What did you eat? What made it special?
- Why do you think Jesus wanted to share a meal with Zacchaeus?
- How has Jesus been present to you around your meal table?

8. "Understanding that we are the One is a deep and precious truth. Like Zacchaeus, Jesus knows your name. Don't miss that! *Jesus knows you.* You are the lost sheep that he would leave the ninety-nine to search for. You are the coin of great value that he would tear apart the house to find. And you are the child that he runs to embrace." (page 9)

- When you read the parables of lost things in Luke 15, which of the characters do you most identify with: The woman searching for her coin? The neighbors who come out to celebrate? The lost sheep? The ninety-nine? The shepherd? The lost son? The older brother? The loving father? Explain.
- What does it mean to you that Jesus searches for you, forgives you, and throws a party for you?
- Is it easy or difficult to receive that kind of generous love? Why?

9. "Having others who also are seeking to live in a way that pleases God will help you grow and hold you accountable. It's a beautiful thing to be the One Jesus loves!" (page 9)
    - Why is community important in our walk with Jesus?
    - What are some ways that you are intentional about building community with other believers?
    - What are some ways that you can be intentional about seeking out the lost in your sphere of influence?

10. Wrap up group discussion with these questions:
    - What stood out to you in your study this week?
    - What new insight did you gain about what it means to be the One?

Call to Action and Prayer (5 minutes)

Invite participants to write down in their journals or Bibles one name of a person whom they desperately want to experience the grace and love of Jesus. Encourage them to choose a time of day to pray for this person every single day, asking God to go after him or her—and asking God for the right words or actions that will point him or her toward God.

After the call to action, close by taking prayer requests from participants and leading the group in prayer. Encourage members to participate in the closing prayer by praying aloud for one another and the requests given. Remind participants to pray for one another and their Ones throughout the week.

THE SHEEP

TWO

Leader Prep

Session Goals

Through this session's discussion, participants will:

- discover that they are or were lost sheep,
- learn what it means to care for the least of these, and
- explore how to seek out lost people.

Preparation

- Read chapter 2, "The Sheep," in *The One* by Jim and Jennifer Cowart.
- Read through this session outline in its entirety to familiarize yourself with the material being covered.
- Read and reflect on the following Scriptures: Isaiah 53:6a; Matthew 25:31-46; 28:19-20; Luke 15:1-7; John 3:16-17; James 2:26; Revelation 21:1-2.
- Have a markerboard or large sheet of paper available for recording group members' ideas.
- Have a Bible, paper for taking notes, and a pen or pencil available for every participant.

What You Will Need

- *The One* DVD and DVD player
- Stick-on name tags and markers (if needed)
- Slips of paper and pens
- Extra Bibles

Session Outline

Gathering (3 minutes)

If group members do not know one another well, hand out name tags and markers and ask participants to write their names on the name tags and wear them for the session. When you are ready to begin the session, pray the opening prayer below or a prayer of your own.

Good Shepherd, thank you for coming to rescue us when we run off. Thank you for your reckless love that chases after us at all cost. Thank you for your presence and guidance as we study your word. Teach us how to find lost ones and show them your grace and love; in Jesus's name. Amen.

Warm Up (5 minutes)

Ask participants to write down three words that describe sheep—the first words that come to mind. Give them a minute to write down their words and then ask the following questions:

- What words came to mind?
- Why do you think you chose those descriptions?
- What do we know about how sheep are referred to in the Bible?

Memory Verse (1 minute)

Say aloud together the memory verse for Week 2:

The Sheep

> *"The Son of Man came to seek and to save the lost."*
>
> (Luke 19:10 NIV)

Video (10-12 minutes)
Play the Week 2 video segment on the DVD.

Group Discussion (30-35 minutes)
Video Discussion

- In the video, Anthony shares how Jesus not only saved his marriage but also was the key to everything else in his life falling into place. How has a relationship with Jesus made a difference in your life story? How does your own story help you share with others about the peace and joy that come from a relationship with God?
- In the video, Jim said, "We are called to do life with salty, messy people…people who have not found the peace and joy of following Jesus." Who are some messy, salty people in your life? How would you describe your attitude about going after those who are far from God?
- How can you get into the community or into the lives of others to earn the privilege of sharing your faith?

Book Discussion

We have provided more discussion points than you will have time to include. Beforehand, select those you want to cover, and place a check mark beside them. Page numbers from the book are provided for reference.

1. "[Sheep] are cute and cuddly, but among the members of the animal kingdom, they are not the

sharpest tools in the shed, or at least they don't appear that way. They tend to wander off and get themselves into trouble. They are virtually defenseless without the care of their shepherd. Yet these particular animals are mentioned many times in the Bible and often are used as a metaphor for me and you." (pages 14-15)

- How do you feel about being compared to a sheep?
- Why do you think sheep are used as a metaphor for our relationship with God?
- Read Isaiah 53:6a. When have you felt like a lost sheep in need of a good shepherd to lead you back to safety?

2. On pages 16-17, Jim reminds us that it's not so bad to be a sheep, that we'd rather be a sheep than a goat based on Jesus's parable of the sheep and the goats. "Being called a biblical, metaphorical sheep sure beats being called a biblical, metaphorical goat! In Matthew 25 Jesus describes a chilling scene that's coming in the future judgment of the world." (page 16)

- Read Matthew 25:31-46. How would you summarize what Jesus is trying to say with this illustration?
- What is your gut reaction to the parable of the sheep and the goats?
- Why do you think Jesus spoke so harshly about those who refused to help the least of these?

3. "Often we get our idea of heaven from cartoons—with us floating around with little wings, playing harps from cloud to cloud. That sounds terrible to

The Sheep

me! How boring! No, one day God will bring an end to this broken world and create a brand-new one where Jesus sits on the throne. It's going to be awesome!" (pages 17-18)

- What do you imagine heaven will be like?
- Read Revelation 21:1-2. What do you make of the imagery in these verses?
- What are some other places in Scripture or Christian tradition where we get our ideas about what heaven will be like?

4. "Dead faith does us no good! That's just stale, crusty religion. Jesus wants us to put our faith into action. We've got to walk the walk as well as talk the talk. A primary way we do that is by reaching out to those who are far from God and developing real relationships with them so that we might have the privilege of sharing Christ with them." (pages 20-21)

- What did the "goats" miss out on when they ignored the least of these?
- Read James 2:26. What does this verse tell us about a life of following Jesus?
- How do we put our faith into action—to be sure that we see and are caring for the least of these?

5. "Lost people are important. God loves his sheep, but not only the sheep in his flock called the church. He also loves the sheep who are still out there, lost. He loves the One who has wandered away. He loves the One who doesn't even know he or she is lost. And he wants us to love them, too, and go find them!" (page 21)

- Read John 3:16-17. Why did Jesus come into the world?
- Read Matthew 28:19-20. What is Jesus calling us to do in these verses? What is this passage usually called by the church?
- What does the phrase "found people find people" mean? Why is this an important task for all believers?

6. "The Good Shepherd lays down his life for his sheep. He will fight wolf and lion and bear to the death to protect his sheep. Can you imagine Jesus feeling that way about you? He does! And he also feels that way about the people around you who don't yet have a relationship with him." (page 24)
    - How have you known Jesus as your Good Shepherd?
    - How can we share the love and rescue of Jesus with those who don't yet have a relationship with him?
    - What are some examples in your life of lost people being found?

7. "This is the message Jesus wants everyone in his audience to understand. Every sheep in the flock has value. Those close to him and those who are living far away." (page 26)
    - What does it mean to you that every sheep in the flock has value?
    - Would you say that you look at others with that same idea? Why or why not?
    - How can your faith community build a culture where everyone who encounters your community knows that they are valued and treasured by Jesus?

8. "Jesus knew that he had two audiences listening to him in the crowd that day.... To the sinners who knew they were sinners: You are the Ones I'm looking for. You are lost and are precious to me. I'm searching for you! To the religious folks: You are lost and don't know it. Follow me! My mission is to seek and save the lost. Come join me in my mission! Help me find the Ones who are lost." (page 26)

    - Read Luke 15:1-7. How does the parable of the lost sheep speak to both the sinners who knew they were sinners and to the religious folks? What is Jesus's message to both groups?
    - Do you see yourself as more of a sheep or a religious folk today? What is Jesus saying to you?
    - How are we to help Jesus find the ones who are lost?

9. "Our primary purpose on earth is to love God and love others. There will never be a more noble goal for your life than sharing Christ with those who don't yet know him." (page 28)

    - How often do you invite someone to worship or a church event?
    - Do you find it easy or difficult to invite others to worship? Why?
    - How can you build or enhance a culture of invitation and welcome at your church?

10. Wrap up group discussion with these questions:

    - What stood out to you in your study this week?
    - What new insight did you gain about what it means to be a sheep of the Good Shepherd?

Call to Action and Prayer (5 minutes)

Invite participants to close their eyes as you guide them in a prayer practice. Say the following phrases slowly, with time for silence between phrases. Ask the group to meditate on each phrase, repeating it in their hearts and letting the Holy Spirit bring images to their minds.

Jesus, you are the Good Shepherd.
I was lost, but you found me.
Jesus, you call me to care for the least of these.
Because I am found, I will go and find lost Ones.

After the call to action, close by taking prayer requests from participants and leading the group in prayer. Encourage members to participate in the closing prayer by praying aloud for one another and the requests given. Remind participants to pray for one another and their Ones throughout the week.

THE COIN

Leader Prep

Session Goals

Through this session's discussion, participants will:

- remember the sweetness of a life with Jesus,
- explore the heart of God for the lost ones in our world, and
- consider who the lost ones are and how we can love them well.

Preparation

- Read chapter 3, "The Coin," in *The One* by Jim and Jennifer Cowart.
- Read through this session outline in its entirety to familiarize yourself with the material being covered.
- Read and reflect on the following Scriptures: Luke 15; 1 Corinthians 1:18; 1 Timothy 6:21; 2 Peter 3:9.
- Have a markerboard or large sheet of paper available for recording group members' ideas.

- Have a Bible, paper for taking notes, and a pen or pencil available for every participant.
- Have blank note cards and envelopes.

What You Will Need

- *The One* DVD and DVD player
- Stick-on name tags and markers (if needed)
- Slips of paper and pens
- Extra Bibles

Session Outline

Gathering (3 minutes)

If desired, hand out name tags and markers and ask participants to write their names on the name tags and wear them for the session. When you are ready to begin the session, pray the opening prayer below or a prayer of your own.

Loving God, thank you for seeking us out. Thank you for loving us more than any worldly treasure. Help us to see the world the way you do, with eyes of compassion and grace. Help us to see those far from you and love them well, always pointing the way to you. Illuminate your word in our conversation today; in Jesus's name. Amen.

Warm Up (5 minutes)

- Did you or do you have a collection of treasures you've collected in your life? Maybe baseball cards, or coins, or spoons, or stickers? What is one of your most treasured items?

Memory Verse (1 minute)

Say aloud together the memory verse for Week 3:

"For where your treasure is, there your heart will be also."

(Matthew 6:21 NIV)

Video (10-12 minutes)

Play the Week 3 video segment on the DVD.

Group Discussion (30-35 minutes)

Video Discussion

- Jim talked about "being committed, maybe obsessed a bit" with reaching the One in your life. What would that look like in your life?
- Jen said, "Sometimes we think we have to make the gospel of Christ attractive to people so they'll be interested." Why do you think we sometimes believe this?
- Jen said, "We have to be willing to be inconvenienced to share Christ." What do you think Jen meant by this?

Book Discussion

We have provided more discussion points and questions than you will have time to include. Beforehand, select those you want to cover, and place a check mark beside them. Page numbers from the book are provided for reference.

1. "We live in a world that suffers from spiritual emptiness. In fact, the things of God often feel like foolishness to people in our society." (page 36)

    - What do you think Jen meant by this statement?
    - When have you felt the world must think you're foolish because of your life with God?
    - Read 1 Corinthians 1:18. What is Paul getting at?

2. "To miss Jesus is to be separated eternally from him. To miss a real relationship with him is to miss heaven. That's not theoretical, it's biblical fact, and it should motivate us to a deep conviction to spend our lives pursuing those who are lost." (page 38)
   - Read 1 Timothy 6:21. What is the most important thing in life?
   - Have you ever had a season when you felt like you were missing the most important things?
   - What do we miss out on when we aren't in relationship with God?

3. "Whether the people in our world suffer as vaccinated Christians or have a view that the things of God are foolishness, our response must be the same. We must seek what is lost. And we must do it with a motivation of love." (page 38)
   - What does Jen mean by the phrase "vaccinated Christians"?
   - What does it mean to seek what is lost?
   - What has been your motivation when you've made attempts at sharing your faith in Jesus?

4. "The point of each of these parables in Luke 15 is to teach the religious folks that everyone has worth." (page 40)
   - Read Luke 15 or review the stories of each of the three parables. What are the objects of worth in each parable? What might the religious folks have thought about the worth of one sheep, a coin, or a wayward son? Why would Jesus want to teach them that everyone has worth?

- What might Jesus be teaching us about what is important?
- What are some of your treasures that wouldn't necessarily be important to anyone else? What would you do if you lost one of them?

5. "There is not a person you will ever meet, not a single one, whom Jesus did not die for." (page 42)

   - Read 2 Peter 3:9. What does this verse tell us about God's heart toward the lost?
   - If we passionately believed that Jesus died for every single person, how would that affect our daily lives?
   - Do you think you would be one to leave the ninety-nine to find the one, or one who stays up all night searching for a treasure? How do we begin to grow that kind of passion for lost things in our hearts?

6. "In Luke 15, we see that the church leaders had gathered to hear Jesus teach, but they had missed the heart of God. The presence of rough folks offended them. The fact that Jesus was developing intimate relationships with these people troubled them even more." (page 42)

   - What are some examples of the church keeping people out? What are some examples of the church reaching out and including everyone?
   - What is the heart of God when it comes to building relationships with "rough folks"?
   - What are some ways to grow our hearts more aligned to God's heart for every single person?

7. "The simple act of friendship is such a powerful way to let people, even those living far outside the bounds of God's law, know that they have value." (page 42)
   - What is one of the most meaningful acts of friendship someone has shown you in your life?
   - Why is a simple act of friendship so powerful?
   - What kinds of acts of friendship might begin relationships with people who don't yet know about God's love or might be hostile to it?

8. "We're all messy people, and every church is filled with sinners. So, go ahead and embrace them no matter what variety they come in. Love them right where they are and then point them to the truth and holiness found in Christ." (page 44)
   - Why do you think the church sometimes gets misunderstood as a bunch of people who have it all together?
   - Would you rather belong to a church that had a safe and clean image to uphold or one that was full of messy, unashamedly imperfect people? Why?
   - How can our churches be more attractive to people on the outside?

9. "It is likely that in order to have the privilege of sharing at any of these levels, you will first need to care for people. Developing real authentic relationships with people is primary to being able to come alongside them to share Jesus. So, consider first how you can demonstrate the love of Christ in practical ways by caring for people,

and then you may have the privilege of eventually sharing Christ with them." (page 45)

- What are some examples in our world of people who showed Jesus's love first by taking care of others?
- Who is being overlooked in our world today? How can your church reach out to those individuals or groups?
- What can you and your congregation do to partner with those desperately in need of the love of Christ?

10. Wrap up group discussion with these questions:

- What stood out to you in your study this week?
- What new insight did you gain about seeking out and caring for the lost ones?

Call to Action and Prayer (3-5 minutes)

Hand out note cards and pens. Invite each participant to write a brief note to someone she or he knows who is far off from God. Suggest that they write a few words about what Jesus means to them, about the grace of God that is freely available, and how they are praying for these persons to come to know the love and joy of life with Jesus. Encourage them to pray about the right time to send their notes or suggest that they may want to use the notes as prompts to pray for the persons every day even if they never send the notes.

After the call to action, close by taking prayer requests from participants and leading the group in prayer. Encourage members to participate in the closing prayer by praying aloud for one another and the requests given. Remind participants to pray for one another and their Ones throughout the week.

THE BOYS

FOUR

Leader Prep

Session Goals

Through this session's discussion, participants will:

- be encouraged toward a passion for reaching lost people,
- explore the story of the lost son, and
- explore the difference between acceptance and approval when it comes to welcoming people.

Preparation

- Read chapter 4, "The Boys," in *The One* by Jim and Jennifer Cowart.
- Read through this session outline in its entirety to familiarize yourself with the material being covered.
- Read and reflect on the following Scriptures: Luke 15 and John 8:3-11.
- Have a markerboard or large sheet of paper available for recording group members' ideas.

- Have a Bible, paper for taking notes, and a pen or pencil available for every participant.

What You Will Need

- *The One* DVD and DVD player
- Stick-on name tags and markers (if needed)
- Slips of paper and pens
- Extra Bibles

Session Outline

Gathering (3 minutes)

If desired, hand out name tags and markers and ask participants to write their names on the name tags and wear them for the session. When you are ready to begin the session, pray the opening prayer below or a prayer of your own.

> *Loving Father, thank you for running out to meet us when we turn to you. Thank you for searching the horizon when we are lost and far from home. Thank you for welcoming us back in your open and loving arms. Teach us how to love like you, to love the lost like you do, and to run after lost people in our world today; in Jesus's name. Amen.*

Warm Up (5 minutes)

- Imagine you are an actor in a movie version of the parable of the two sons. Which role are you playing? Why did you choose this role?

Memory Verse (1 minute)

Say aloud together the memory verse for Week 4:

> *We love because he first loved us.*
> *(1 John 4:19 NIV)*

Video (10-12 minutes)
Play the Week 4 video segment on the DVD.

Group Discussion (30-35 minutes)
Video Discussion
- How does Harry's story about his stepfather pursuing him encourage you to hold on to hope in God—and the hope that you or someone you love can be found? Is there someone you've been disconnected from that you need to reach out to now?
- How does Jim and Jen's explanation of the father's actions in the parable influence or change your perception of God's love for you? for lost people?
- In the video, Jen encouraged believers to adopt the attitude of the father running after the lost son. Who in your life has modeled this passion for reaching those who are far from God? Who has reached out to you personally to tell you about God's love and forgiveness through Christ?

Book Discussion

We have provided more discussion points and questions than you will have time to include. Beforehand, select those you want to cover, and place a check mark beside them. Page numbers from the book are provided for reference.

1. "No one wants to be your little project. No one wants you to try to save them if you aren't willing to really listen and care about them first. It feels icky and insincere. It feels fake and artificial. It feels like the person trying to convert or save you doesn't really care about you at all. It often makes you feel as if you are a part of an agenda, a notch on a belt,

or a check mark on a self-righteous to-do list." (pages 56-57)

- Have you ever felt like you were someone's project? What did that feel like?
- Why is sincerity so important as we share our faith?
- What are some examples from your life of sincere relationships that pointed you in the direction of God?

2. "I would say that sometimes our churches are small and we don't have many friends because we aren't very nice. People like to be around other people who treat us with dignity and respect. We avoid people who come across as judgmental or superior." (page 57)

- What are some ways that Christians have been or maybe even still are perceived?
- Generally, what kind of reputation does the church have in our culture? Why do you think this is so?
- If the church was passionate about lost people, what might its reputation be?

3. "An attitude of superiority was part of the Pharisees' problem in Luke 15. They were convinced that they were better than those in the crowd, and that attitude showed when they interacted with people outside their religious context.... Compassion is key when it comes to sharing the love of Jesus." (pages 57-58)

- Review the details of the three stories of lost things in Luke 15. What do you see about the attitude of the Pharisees as they question Jesus?

- Would you say that you are quicker to judge or to empathize? Explain.
- Jesus always led with compassion. How does one grow compassion for others in their hearts?

4. "[The story of the Lost Son] is not about a lost boy; it's about two lost boys. One is lost in a faraway land. The other is lost at home. One is wild, rowdy, and lost. The other is quiet, cynical, and lost. One is far from God because of selfish desires. The other is far from God because of selfish hypocrisy." (page 69)

- What did you think about the "movie version" of the parable from chapter 4? Did Jim get the actors right? What would you change about the cast?
- How did reading the story like a movie reveal new insights about what Jesus might have been trying to communicate in the parable?
- Why do you think the prodigal son is most known in the story when the other son had plenty of his own issues we can relate to?

5. "People can be lost a thousand miles away, but they can also be lost sitting on a velvety cushioned pew." (page 70)

- Which brother do you most relate to? Why?
- What does Jim mean by the statement that people can be lost far away or lost sitting in church?
- Have you ever felt lost, even when you're sitting in church? What was it like to be found by God?

6. "Jesus helps us see a new, more accurate image of God—a God who does something many would

consider undignified: he runs to those he loves! God is filled with compassion and mercy, and his heart aches for those who are lost. So he runs to us, and then, when we are found, he issues an invitation: *Come run with me!*" (page 70)

- What did you think about God's heart toward sinners before you came to know Jesus?
- How does the father in the parable of the lost son teach us about the heart of God toward lost people?
- Have you ever thought of the Great Commandment—to love God and love others—as an invitation to run toward the lost? What do you think about that invitation?

7. "There are people around you—friends, family, and people you will pass on the street today—who are lost. Some are engaged in wild living and haven't been to church in years, if ever. Many of them believe that God does not love or care for them because they haven't experienced love from the ones who represent him on earth, the church people. They haven't yet experienced the love of the God who runs." (page 71)

- How can we imitate the love of a God who runs after us?
- What is the feeling of coming home to a loving God? How can we talk about that invitation in compelling ways to folks who haven't yet come home to God?
- What could you do to lead the way at your church in creating a culture of welcome and invitation?

8. "As you seek to reach the Ones in your life, remember that there is a huge difference between acceptance and approval. You can love, seek, and run to very messy people without putting a stamp of approval on their sinful behaviors. Loving and accepting people right where they are is what we're called to do. I often tell our congregation, 'Everyone is welcome—we will love you right where you are. But we will love you deeply enough to tell you the truth from God's Word.'" (page 71)

   - Do you ever get tripped up on the difference between acceptance and approval? How so?
   - How did the father in the story of the lost son accept the son, but not approve of the behavior?
   - Read John 8:3-11. How did Jesus accept the woman but not her behavior?

9. "In accepting people, we offer both grace and truth in large measures but do not approve or condone sinful behaviors. Like everything else, this takes practice. We need to practice it individually and corporately as the church." (pages 72-73)

   - Why is it so important to serve grace and truth in large measure as we run toward the lost?
   - How can we practice grace as we accept people and also speak the truth in love when we need to?
   - What does it mean that our churches should be both a "fortress of the saints" and an "ER for the injured"?

10. Wrap up group discussion with these questions:
    - What stood out to you in your study this week?

- What new insight did you gain about what it means to run toward the lost?

Call to Action and Prayer (3-5 minutes)

Invite participants to sketch out a line drawing of your sanctuary. Ask them to bring to mind some names of lost people in their lives—the Ones who know they're lost and the Ones who don't. As the names come to mind, have participants write those names on the sketch of the sanctuary as a way of praying that God would run to them and bring them home. Encourage the group to keep this drawing and pray continually for these friends to come home.

After the call to action, close by taking prayer requests from the participants and leading the group in prayer. Encourage members to participate in the closing prayer by praying aloud for one another and the requests given. Remind participants to continue praying for one another and their Ones throughout the weeks and months to come. Set a date for your group to check back in, maybe a month or two down the road, to get an update on how your new passion for reaching lost Ones is going. Celebrate those who have come home and add to your list new people you've met whom you long to bring to Jesus.

Resources for a Church-wide Emphasis

REACHING THE ONE: OVERCOMING OBSTACLES

> *If the ax is dull*
> *and its edge unsharpened,*
> *more strength is needed,*
> *but skill will bring success.*
> *(Ecclesiastes 10:10 NIV)*

As a child of God, most likely you already buy into the idea of an evangelistic life emphasis, even a church-wide culture dedicated to reaching the Ones in your community. But the question lingers, *How do we get started?*

So often our hearts are eager to serve, to reach, and to love those around us in Jesus's name, but how do we do that effectively in our various contexts? People have written many books on *why* we should be active in living out the Great Commission, but *how* we do that can be challenging. We need to develop and continue to refine the skills necessary to reach those far from Christ in our local areas of influence.

The materials that follow are some ideas that you may want to consider as you develop a plan to become even more intentional in living out the Great Commission in real and vital ways. They have worked in our local setting, and we believe they can help you too. Our hope is that you will take these strategies and adapt them for your situation. The goal is to become consistently focused on reaching those far from God. Actually developing systems that perpetuate a culture of invitation and welcome is the ultimate end.

Ideally, this can be done on a church-wide level, but it is best lived out in personal ways. So, if you do not have the authority to institute church-wide change, then implement where you can. A Sunday school class, small group, Bible study group, youth group, or even just a group of friends can commit to using many of these principles to develop strategies to live into the Great Commission in effective ways.

Before we get into *how* to create a church-wide synergy around evangelism, we want to encourage you not to become discouraged when you see ideas that will be challenging in your setting.

Every new venture has challenges. You will face roadblocks. Barriers will stand in your way, so before you read further, we hope you will choose an attitude of "how do we make this work?" as opposed to "this won't work." Begin to meditate on what's possible as opposed to what stands in your way.

Overcoming your obstacles will be key to effectiveness in instituting real change. In our leadership book *Start This, Stop That* (Abingdon Press) we share about the practice of overcoming obstacles.

> One of our kids' favorite games is what we call "So/But." Here's how it works. We begin a story with "so," such as, "So, I was going to the greatest toy store ever to buy you a gift, but..."
>
> Then one of the kids takes over: "But, there was a giant gorilla wearing lipstick that tried to attack me, so..."
>
> It's my turn again: "So, I became a ninja warrior and attacked that giant gorilla, but..."

Then the kids throw me another obstacle: "But the gorilla had studied karate under Chuck Norris and your ninja warrior skills were of no use, so…"

On and on it goes until finally we overcome all of their obstacles and accomplish the goal.

In ministry you are going to have obstacles. Jesus told us, "In this world you will have trouble. But take heart! I have overcome the world" (John 16:33 NIV). You are going to have obstacles in life. These are your Buts. Some of you have some big Buts in your lives right now: "I'd like to reach out to the unchurched, *but* my congregation doesn't seem to care." "We would love to have a dynamic children's program, *but* no one will volunteer to lead it." On and on it goes. Move past the excuses and change the conjunction. Instead of saying *but*, say *so*. For example, "The congregation has not been excited about reaching out to the unchurched, *so* our next sermon series is focused on the Great Commission and what God is calling us to do in our area." The So helps move the congregation past the paralysis caused by the giant, pink-lipstick-wearing gorilla in the room to a stage of problem solving.

As Harvest experienced rapid growth, we had no space to accommodate large numbers of children. We were meeting in a theater and had a limited number of spaces. One weekend we had more than fifty children in one classroom-type setting. At best it was controlled chaos. So, we had to come up with a new way of doing Christian education. The traditional Sunday school setting would not work. Out of necessity, we assessed our options and created what we call the "carpet group system." Instead of having each theater accommodate one group in a classroom-type setting, we put down different colored carpets and assigned eight to twelve children per carpet with a leader. Using this system, we were able to grow in the same space to handle 250 children at once.

Instead of giving up, when faced with a big But, we kept struggling until we discovered a So. It has worked. In fact, as we designed our new facility, we chose to keep our carpet system. (This decision saved us millions of dollars, by the way.)

All too often, when we encounter obstacles, we are overwhelmed. Instead of facing the obstacle with faith, tenacity, and creativity, we allow the obstacle to win. When Moses led the Hebrew people across the desert to the promised land, do you remember what happened? "This was their report to Moses: 'We arrived in the land you sent us to see, and it is indeed a magnificent country—a land flowing with milk and honey.... But the people living there are powerful....' They spread discouraging reports" (Num. 13:27-28, 32 NLT 1996). When ten of the twelve spies faced a significant obstacle, they not only were afraid but also panicked the people. An entire generation missed the promised land because ten spies got stuck on the But. An entire generation missed the blessing God had for them because a few people would not face their obstacle, which basically was fear. Only Caleb and Joshua said, So "if the LORD is pleased with us...they are only helpless prey to us! They have no protection....Don't be afraid of them!" (Num. 14:8-9 NLT). When we look beyond the obstacle, we can move in faith.

To be clear: the Buts in your life are real. You have to face them and find ways of dealing with them.

There really were giants in Canaan; however, with God's help, Joshua and Caleb led a faithful generation to defeat them. Basically, we have two options as we face the future: fear or faith. An attitude of fear will give in to the obstacles. An attitude of faith will not give up until the obstacle has been overcome.

While consulting with a church in eastern Kentucky, we were presented with a challenge. Children no longer attended the church. Once we did the research, we discovered there were plenty of children in the area, but on Sunday mornings in that particular area, many children helped their parents with crops in the field. It was a relatively poor area, and on the weekend, during daylight hours, the entire family helped bring in the harvest. The church had a real But to face. "We would like to have children in our church, but they are busy on Sunday mornings." We helped them move toward a So: "So, move your programming to a weekday evening, and prepare a meal for the whole family." At first, some of the church folks complained because that was not their usual church time. It seemed an inconvenience to some members. To this pastor's credit, she did it anyway, and it worked.[1]

So, as you begin to dream about implementing strategies to reach those far from God, you will come against obstacles. That's just part of the journey. *Don't give up too quickly!* Some of the "buts" you face may include criticism, lack of support, unenthusiastic leadership, fear, and financial limitations. These are real and will need to be addressed. But don't let them stop you!

1. Jennifer Cowart and Jim Cowart, *Start This, Stop That: Do the Things That Grow Your Church* (Nashville: Abingdon Press, 2012), 17–19.

First, we will address those of you who would NOT identify yourself as a leader in a local church setting—even if you might lead or facilitate a small group. Then we will address church leaders.

Reaching the One Outside a Leadership Role

As you think about how to become active in reaching the lost, you may think, *"But I'm not a leader. I don't have a title or position in my local church."* Don't allow that to keep you from actively seeking to reach the lost in your sphere of influence. Leadership is all about influence—no title necessary. So, if you come in contact with other humans, then you have the potential for influence, which means you can be a leader at a personal level.

Honestly, the most success I (Jen) personally have had in leading people to Jesus is from the stage, but getting them into the doors of the church has happened at a much more personal level. It's doing things like stopping to talk to the lady at the dry cleaner or inviting the guy who helps me get the groceries into the car. It's looking for the moving van in the neighborhood and letting new people know we'd like to get to know them. It's developing relationships with neighbors, the families of my kids' classmates, and people I meet at the gym. By taking time to personally connect with people, you earn the privilege to then begin a relationship that ultimately may lead to the honor of sharing Jesus with them, or at least inviting them to church with you.

In my experience, an effective way to connect with people far from God is to lean in when you realize they are hurting. When people are in pain, they are more likely to share their story. When I see that pain with friends, acquaintances, and even strangers, I'll often ask two simple questions:

1. What's going on?
2. How can I pray for you?

When I ask people if I can pray for them, I've noticed that no one has ever turned me down. Even if they don't believe in God! I guess they figure, *Well, if you're praying anyway, go ahead and include me/my marriage/my kids/my sickness—whatever.* Probably they are thinking, *Well, who knows, it couldn't hurt, I guess.* The point is that it opens a door for them to know that I love the Lord and I care about them. Both are important.

If it's appropriate, then I follow up with two more things:

1. What can I do to help?
2. I'd love for you to join me at church this week.

When you eat out, go to the gym, sit in the carpool line, go to the park, wherever, be ready to invite. Have your strategy ready and make it a practice to pray every morning, asking God to use you to share his love with those you meet. If you pray that in sincerity, you'll begin to see new opportunities around every corner, and it's exciting!

Reaching the One within a Leadership Role

Now, if you are a leader in the local church setting, your role is to help people move past their objections (buts) when it comes to living out Christ's commands. Here are three practical ways to help others move past their roadblocks:

1. Cast compelling biblical vision.
2. Pray.
3. Lead by example.

If you are the pastor, preach the vision. If you are a group leader, cast a fresh and compelling picture of what it would be like to live on mission with God, reaching out to those who don't yet know him. The more clearly you are able to cast a clear biblical vision of a preferred future, the more likely it is that you will be able to achieve it. As you share this goal of being evangelistically alive, pray. Really pray. Ask God for clarity, wisdom, and breakthrough for a community-wide movement of life change. Then, just do it. Lead by example. If you want people to invite, become a champion inviter. If you want to see first-time guests, then start being the one to bring people with you to church and small group. Don't wait for a committee to vote or a steering team to plan. Just do it. Live into the Great Commission with abandon and watch God show up!

PLANNING A CHURCH-WIDE EMPHASIS

In our setting, we call a church-wide emphasis a campaign, but we hesitate to use that word because it is so often associated with a fund-raising movement. So, we suggest making the mental shift from using the word *campaign* to using *emphasis*, describing a broader multifaceted approach to creating a culture and even a movement that gets people working together toward a common goal.

At Harvest, we create a church-wide emphasis about twice a year. The emphasis varies, but the goals are the same: move people in the same direction, encourage them to join small groups, grow their faith, and give them something compelling to which they would want to invite their friends.

Themes we have used in the past have included: Here, Near and Far—a church on mission; If These Walls Could Talk—living out faith in your home; Big Questions—an apologetics series; Living the Five—implementing the five commands contained in the Great Commission and Great Commandment; and obviously, The One—a call to reaching those close to us who don't know Jesus. The topics of an emphasis may vary, but the basic components are consistent: Weekend

Messages, Small Group Materials, Prayer Support, Memory Verses, and Invitational Tools. (These will be discussed later in this chapter.)

Benefits of a Church-wide Emphasis

As you plan and create your church-wide emphasis to reach the One, you will have the opportunity to:

- cast fresh, compelling vision;
- brand your message within the church and community;
- teach biblical truths in creatively redundant fashion;
- stir up synergy among believers;
- motivate people to new behavior;
- move people into small groups; and
- give believers an "event" to invite their nonbelieving friends to attend.

In Acts we see the early church model the multifaceted approach of ministry. Many of the components of the emphasis are embedded in this powerful passage:

> **Everyone was filled with awe** at the many **wonders and signs** performed by the apostles. All the **believers were together** and had everything in common. They sold property and possessions to **give to anyone** who had need. Every day **they continued to meet together in the temple** courts. They **broke bread** in **their homes** and ate together with glad and sincere hearts, praising God and enjoying the favor of all the people. And **the Lord added to their number daily** those who were being saved.
>
> (Acts 2:43-47 NIV, emphasis added)

- filled with awe—an excitement about what was happening
- wonders and signs—God moving miraculously in their midst
- believers were together—unity and synergy of a common goal
- giving to those in need—meeting practical needs in the community
- met together in the temple—corporate worship with purpose and passion
- broke bread—sharing Communion and eating together
- met in homes—small group fellowship
- the Lord added to their number daily—people saved on a daily basis!

As we read about how the early church functioned, we see many moving parts at work here. Each one contributed to the overall health and growth of the family of God. In essence, it was a Holy Spirit-driven emphasis!

Components of a Church-wide Emphasis

As you begin creating an evangelistic emphasis for your community, here are some basic components to consider:

Weekend Services

The weekend service is meant to be a gathering filled with passion, praise, prayer, and a powerful message, giving hope and direction to those who are gathered.

If you are the pastor of the church, your single greatest tool to reach people and cast a clear compelling vision for reaching the One will come through the weekend service. Instead of asking a board or committee to vote on whether or not to live into the Great Commission, preach through it!

People are hungry for godly leaders who will come forward and lead in clear, compelling ways. We need pastors in local churches who will stand up and share from God's Word the direction that Jesus intends his church to go.

As we read the psalms, we see that there is great emotion in worshipping the Lord. Singing, praising, music, even dancing are present. There seems to be an atmosphere of celebration and joy. As we see the early church assemble in the New Testament, there is a passionate dedication to the mission of the church. The goal is to assemble not only for fellowship but also for prayer and a dedication to the purposes of God. People are generally very excited to follow a leader who has a clear, compelling vision that is rooted in God's Word.

As you craft weekend messages, make sure that you are clear and concise. Be sure that people can see where you're leading and what their role in that journey will be. Each week during the church-wide emphasis, you may want to have one clear action step for people to take.

For instance:

- **Week 1**: Identify five people in your life who don't yet have a relationship with Jesus.
- **Week 2**: Begin to pray for your five people. Also begin to pray for the courage to take the step of invitation next week.
- **Week 3**: Invite your five to church (or to a nonthreatening event such as a block party).
- **Week 4**: Meet your One or Ones at church and take them to lunch afterward.

As you lead, remember to stay very close to Jesus. Stay humble. Pray and seek God's guidance as you prepare the weekend message, or the Sunday school lesson, or whatever your role may be. Be clear. Be concise. Stay focused on the One.

If you are the pastor, your roles can be numerous and demanding: counseling the troubled, visiting the sick, caring for the elderly, handling daily church concerns. But do not forget that a primary task of the pastor is to feed and to lead. If the tasks of the church outside of preaching and leading are consuming your time, then you may need to make your first step empowering laity to take on these tasks within the church family. The biblical model teaches us that the pastor is to equip the saints for the working of ministry. They have spiritual gifts and abilities that need to be activated, and when that happens, pastors are freed up to spend more time crafting sermons and creating ministry strategies.

As you specifically begin to prepare messages for the One, keep these verses before you daily and let them guide you:

> [37]"'Love the Lord your God with all your heart and with all your soul and with all your mind.' [38]This is the first and greatest commandment. [39]And the second is like it: 'Love your neighbor as yourself.'"
> (Matthew 22:37-39 NIV)

> [19]"Therefore go and make disciples of all nations, baptizing them in the name of the Father and of the Son and of the Holy Spirit, [20]and teaching them to obey everything I have commanded you. And surely I am with you always, to the very end of the age."
> (Matthew 28:19-20 NIV)

If you are a leader at any level, keep these tips in mind as you cast vision:

- Consistently share the vision in creatively redundant ways. Once or twice is not enough.
- Be clear and concise.
- Give specific action steps.
- Leverage influence with other leaders by having meetings before the meeting.
- Use meetings as vision-casting sessions and not just occasions to give reports.
- Be gentle, but bold.
- Love everyone and be kind to all, but move forward with those who catch the vision.

Small Groups

The early church met in homes for fellowship, Communion, and to share life together. In that same fashion, a powerful component of the church-wide emphasis is the small group experience. Activating every attender into a cell group for the purpose of focusing on reaching those far from Christ will help build momentum and synergy.

In our leadership book, *Grab, Gather, Grow* (G3) (Abingdon Press, 2012), we share our learnings about creating a system that involves the entire church family in small group life. Through the G3 process, in fact, at times we have more people in weekly groups than we have in weekend attendance—a feat that we, honestly, had not believed possible. There are many benefits to a strong small group system, which include membership care, spiritual maturity, developing more intimate friendships, and casting vision in smaller settings. But an additional benefit in *The One* will be the members' ability to process verbally their fears about reaching out to friends and family who don't yet know Christ. These fears are real, and if people are really going to engage, they'll need to process those concerns so they can move into action.

In order to facilitate your small group strategy in conjunction with *The One*, provide your people with the discussion questions and exercises in this book, as well as the video segments on the accompanying DVD, to help engage them in directed conversation. Preparing your church-wide emphasis in advance and pairing these materials with the weekend service can be a powerful tool. The idea is to mirror information from the weekend while providing fresh Scripture, insights, and discussion questions. We call this creative redundancy: the points are basically the same from the weekend to the small group, but expressed in new and varying ways.

Creating this system is best done with the lead pastor personally involved. It can be delegated, but if the pastor does not drive the vision from the stage/pulpit, it will be much harder to achieve church-wide engagement.

In our experience, the weekend service and the small group experience are the two most critical pieces to implementing a successful church-wide emphasis.

Memory Verses

This is a simple step to implement. In fact, at the end of each of the four chapters in the participant book, we have included a memory verse. The verses are also included in this leader guide (see page 77). The memory verses are one more way to drive home the passion and scriptural mandate for us to be active in reaching the One.

Prayer Support

Turning your congregation into a well-organized evangelistic engine is sure to draw the attention of the enemy. So, be proactive by covering the entire effort from start to finish in prayer. Think about tackling this on several fronts rather than with just one effort. Here are a few ideas:

- **The One prayer team**—Include people dedicated to praying daily.
- **Church-wide prayer emphasis**—Pray for one another to have the courage to reach out to those far from God.
- **Around-the-clock prayer vigil**—Have church members sign up for shifts so that people are praying continually during week 3 for members to reach out to those far from God and invite them to "come and see" as Philip urged Nathaniel to do in John 1.
- **Personal emphasis**—Every week, encourage members to focus on the appropriate action step: identify their Ones, pray for their Ones, share their faith and invite their Ones, and plan to meet them at church and invite them to lunch.

Before, during, and after the church-wide emphasis, soak all that you do in prayer. We know that God wants us to be passionate about reaching out to people far from him, and we will need his help and wisdom to do that effectively. This is a great way to gather a team to cast vision and get them actively engaged before the church-wide emphasis even gets started.

Branding

Creating a cohesive message within the church will help build momentum as your church-wide emphasis progresses. You're welcome to use the graphics provided at www.abingdonpress.com/theonedownloads or create your own. Give the series an identity so that it takes on a life of its own. And then…put it everywhere. T-shirts, social media, the church website and newsletter, the walls of the church, the front of the bulletin, inserts—keep the emphasis in front of people to create a sense of urgency and excitement.

Skills Training

People may need coaching about how to share Christ, how to invite people to church, and how to pray for the Ones in their lives who don't yet know him. Don't assume that they already have these skills. Use humor, video, and skits to model how to be invitational in winsome ways. Many people are afraid of sharing their faith or even inviting people to church. By modeling easy-to-use techniques and conversation starters, you can make the process less scary and more attainable.

Another skill you may want to teach is how to develop meaningful, genuine, and authentic relationships with those far from Christ. No one wants to feel like a project, so some helpful coaching in this area may be wise.

Invitational Tools

Help your people win by giving them the tools they need be successful. Developing events and distributing materials they can use as invitations will increase the chances that they will become effective inviters. Here are a few ideas:

- Create invitations that can be handed out at school, work, and in neighborhoods.
- Put out video invitations that can be shared on social media.
- Host community-wide events that hold interest for nonbelievers, such as a fish fry, concert, block party, kids' festival, and so on.

WEEKLY MEMORY VERSES

Week 1

"Believe in the Lord Jesus, and you will be saved."
(Acts 16:31 NIV)

Week 2

"The Son of Man came to seek and to save the lost."
(Luke 19:10 NIV)

Week 3

"For where your treasure is, there your heart will be also."
(Matthew 6:21 NIV)

Week 4

We love because he first loved us.
(1 John 4:19 NIV)

WEEKLY SERMON STARTERS

Week 1: You Are the One

Primary Scripture Focus:

> ¹*Tax collectors and other notorious sinners often came to listen to Jesus teach.* ²*This made the Pharisees and teachers of religious law complain that he was associating with such sinful people—even eating with them!*
>
> *(Luke 15:1-2)*

Sermon Points

1. Jesus had a specific mission from God.

    "For the Son of Man came to seek and save those who are lost."
    (Luke 19:10)

    "For God so loved the world that he gave his one and only Son, that whoever believes in him shall not perish but have eternal life."
    (John 3:16 NIV)

2. As Christ-followers, we have been given the same mission.

> *"Therefore, go and make disciples of all the nations, baptizing them in the name of the Father and the Son and the Holy Spirit."*
> *(Matthew 28:19)*

3. Your life is better when you live on mission with Jesus.

> *"But seek first his kingdom and his righteousness, and all these things will be given to you as well."*
> *(Matthew 6:33 NIV)*

4. "Non-church people" were, and are, drawn to Jesus.

5. Jesus loves being with "the One."

6. In modern times, Christ-followers have built barriers between ourselves and "the One"—busyness, fear, apathy.

7. A functioning addict is one who hides his or her addiction so well that he or she can function in society undetected; no one knows about the addiction. A functioning Christian is one who hides his or her faith so well that they can function in society undetected; no one knows about their faith.

Sermon Questions:
- Do we really take the Bible seriously?
- Do we really take the mission personally?
- Do we really care about the One?

Week 2: The Sheep

Primary Scripture Focus:

> [4]"If a man has a hundred sheep and one of them gets lost, what will he do? Won't he leave the ninety-nine others in the wilderness and go to search for the one that is lost until he finds it? [5]And when he has found it, he will joyfully carry it home on his shoulders. [6]When he arrives, he will call together his friends and neighbors, saying, 'Rejoice with me because I have found my lost sheep.' [7]In the same way, there is more joy in heaven over one lost sinner who repents and returns to God than over ninety-nine others who are righteous and haven't strayed away!"
>
> (Luke 15:4-7)

Sermon Points

1. Jesus has a mission from God: to *seek and save* the lost.

   > "For the Son of Man came to seek and save those who are lost."
   >
   > (Luke 19:10)

2. God has given this same mission to *every Christ-follower*.

   > [18]Then Jesus came to them and said, "All authority in heaven and on earth has been given to me. [19]Therefore go and make disciples of all nations, baptizing them in the name of the Father and of the Son and of the Holy Spirit, [20]and teaching them to obey everything I have commanded you. And surely I am with you always, to the very end of the age."
   >
   > (Matthew 28:18-20 NIV)

3. Our lives have more purpose and meaning when we live *on mission* with God.

   "But seek first his kingdom and his righteousness, and all these things will be given to you as well."
   (Matthew 6:33 NIV)

4. In this parable, there are two categories of people: lost and found/safe/secure.

   - Lostness implies value. Lost people are incredibly valuable to God.
   - Every number represents a name. Every name has a story. Every story is someone Jesus died for.

5. Lost sheep have no direction.

   We all, like sheep, have gone astray,
   *   each of us has turned to our own way.*
   (Isaiah 53:6a NIV)

   Prone to wander, Lord, I feel it,
   *   prone to leave the God I love;*
   here's my heart, O take and seal it,
   *   seal it for thy courts above.*
   (Robert Robinson, "Come, Thou Fount of Every Blessing," 1758)

6. Lost sheep have no protection.

   "Therefore the people wander like sheep oppressed for lack of a shepherd.
   (Zechariah 10:2b NIV)

   The Lord is my shepherd, I lack nothing.
   (Psalm 23:1 NIV)

   "I [Jesus] am the good shepherd. The good shepherd lays down his life for the sheep."
   (John 10:11 NIV)

7. It's easy for us to relate to the lost sheep because we have a tendency to wander. But God wants us to imitate the Shepherd.

Jesus said, "Then feed my sheep."
(John 21:17b)

Sermon Questions:

- Are we prone to wander?
- Are we seeking first the kingdom of God?
- Do we really care about the One?

Week Three: The Coin

Primary Scripture Focus:

[8]"Or suppose a woman has ten silver coins and loses one. Won't she light a lamp and sweep the entire house and search carefully until she finds it? [9]And when she finds it, she will call in her friends and neighbors and say, 'Rejoice with me because I have found my lost coin.' [10]In the same way, there is joy in the presence of God's angels when even one sinner repents."

(Luke 15:8-10)

Sermon Points

1. Jesus has a mission from God: to seek and save the lost.

    "For the Son of Man came to seek and save those who are lost."

    (Luke 19:10)

2. God has given this same mission to every Christ-follower.

    [18]Then Jesus came to them and said, "All authority in heaven and on earth has been given to me. [19]Therefore go and make disciples of all nations, baptizing them in the name of the Father and of the Son and of the Holy Spirit, [20]and teaching them to obey everything I have commanded you. And surely I am with you always, to the very end of the age."

    (Matthew 28:18-20 NIV)

3. Our lives have more purpose and meaning when we live on mission with God.

"But seek first his kingdom and his righteousness, and all these things will be given to you as well."
(Matthew 6:33 NIV)

4. The lost coin isn't worthless; its value is just wasted.

5. When I'm disconnected from God, that's what it means to be spiritually lost.

6. Why the passionate search for the coin?

7. value = a day's wage

    - ten silver coins of a married woman's headdress

8. She doesn't just rejoice privately; she calls together her friends and neighbors to invite them to share in her joy. What was lost has been found!

9. Are we throwing parties for the lost who have been found?

    - Where does that kind of passion come from?

Sermon Questions:

- Who is your One?

Week Four: The Boys

Primary Scripture Focus:

> [11]To illustrate the point further, Jesus told them this story: "A man had two sons. [12]The younger son told his father, 'I want my share of your estate now before you die.' So his father agreed to divide his wealth between his sons.
>
> [13]"A few days later this younger son packed all his belongings and moved to a distant land, and there he wasted all his money in wild living. [14]About the time his money ran out, a great famine swept over the land, and he began to starve. [15]He persuaded a local farmer to hire him, and the man sent him into his fields to feed the pigs. [16]The young man became so hungry that even the pods he was feeding the pigs looked good to him. But no one gave him anything.
>
> [17]"When he finally came to his senses, he said to himself, 'At home even the hired servants have food enough to spare, and here I am dying of hunger! [18]I will go home to my father and say, "Father, I have sinned against both heaven and you, [19]and I am no longer worthy of being called your son. Please take me on as a hired servant."'
>
> [20]"So he returned home to his father. And while he was still a long way off, his father saw him coming. Filled with love and compassion, he ran to his son, embraced him, and kissed him. [21]His son said to him, 'Father, I have sinned against both heaven and you, and I am no longer worthy of being called your son.'

²²"But his father said to the servants, 'Quick! Bring the finest robe in the house and put it on him. Get a ring for his finger and sandals for his feet. ²³And kill the calf we have been fattening. We must celebrate with a feast, ²⁴for this son of mine was dead and has now returned to life. He was lost, but now he is found.' So the party began.

²⁵"Meanwhile, the older son was in the fields working. When he returned home, he heard music and dancing in the house, ²⁶and he asked one of the servants what was going on. ²⁷'Your brother is back,' he was told, 'and your father has killed the fattened calf. We are celebrating because of his safe return.'

²⁸"The older brother was angry and wouldn't go in. His father came out and begged him, ²⁹but he replied, 'All these years I've slaved for you and never once refused to do a single thing you told me to. And in all that time you never gave me even one young goat for a feast with my friends. ³⁰Yet when this son of yours comes back after squandering your money on prostitutes, you celebrate by killing the fattened calf!'

³¹"His father said to him, 'Look, dear son, you have always stayed by me, and everything I have is yours. ³²We had to celebrate this happy day. For your brother was dead and has come back to life! He was lost, but now he is found!'"
(Luke 15:11-32)

Sermon Points

1. In all of these lost stories, religious people are shocked that Jesus says God loves and searches for lost people.

"For the Son of Man came to seek and save those who are lost."

(Luke 19:10)

2. The younger son says, "I won't change until I get fed up with my life."

   ¹³*"He wasted all his money....* ¹⁴*His money ran out....* ¹⁶*The young man became so hungry....* ¹⁷**He finally came to his senses."**
   (Luke 15:13-17, emphasis added)

   *"When you come looking for me, you'll find me. / Yes, when you get serious about finding **me** and want it more than anything else, I'll make sure you won't be disappointed."*
   (Jeremiah 29:13 MSG, emphasis added)

3. The younger son had to own up to his own sin.

   ¹⁷*"When he finally came to his senses...* ¹⁸*I have sinned against both heaven and you."*
   (Luke 15:17-18)

   *"But **if we confess our sins** to him [God], he is faithful and just to forgive us our sins and to cleanse us from all wickedness."*
   (1 John 1:9, emphasis added)

4. The younger son had to give himself to God.

   "I am no longer worthy of being called your son. Please take me on as a hired servant."
   (Luke 15:19)

   Give your bodies to God.... Let them be a living and holy sacrifice—the kind he will find acceptable. This is truly the way to worship him.
   (Romans 12:1)

5. The older son became unconcerned for his lost brother.

   ²⁹*"These many years I have been serving you.... ³⁰But as soon as this son of yours came...you killed the fatted calf."*
   (Luke 15:29-30 NKJV)

6. The older son felt entitled.

   ²⁸*"But he [older son] was angry and would not go in.... ²⁹You never gave me a young goat."*
   (Luke 15:28-29 NKJV)

7. The older son became unresponsive.

   - The story ends abruptly. We aren't told if the older brother is convinced and comes into the celebration or if he remains outside, angry and discontented.

Sermon Questions:

- What happens when we refuse to obey?
- Why are both sons loved by the father?
- Who is your One? Are you the One?

A FINAL WORD OF ENCOURAGEMENT

Just this week a friend dropped by the office and asked, "When will we do 'The One' series again? It was my favorite thing we have ever done as a church." I said, "Well, that was a one-time series, with a long-term emphasis." Her response was, "No, let's do it again—and again—and again. Every year we need a refresher course to help us remember that this is why Jesus leaves us here. To love, invite, and reach those who don't know him yet." It was encouraging to hear her enthusiasm and to realize how deeply "The One" series had touched her life. I was reminded of several Scriptures as she was speaking:

> *Always be prepared to give an answer to everyone who asks you to give the reason for the hope that you have. But do this with gentleness and respect.*
> *(1 Peter 3:15 NIV)*

> *Do your best to present yourself to God as one approved, a worker who has no need to be ashamed, rightly handling the word of truth.*
> *(2 Timothy 2:15 ESV)*

The One

"Go into all the world and preach the Good News to everyone."

(Mark 16:15)

How encouraging to hear that our people are eager to continue to be about the work of reaching those far from Christ! In fact, they not only want their church to be known for caring for the One, but they want to be individually known for it as well.

So what have the results been in our situation as we focused on the One? At Harvest, we have seen a dramatic increase in first-time visitors, which has resulted in a renewed number of first-time decisions to follow Jesus.

God loves people. So much so that he allowed Jesus to suffer on the cross for us. He longs to have a relationship with us now and forevermore. But his love is not just for us. We are already in his family. He wants us to grow that family. Living into the Great Commandment by loving God and others and sharing the message of Jesus with others are the most important things we will do on this planet. It should actually consume us! We hope that the passion to reach the One will grow within you and within your community. May God bless you as you seek him and as you share his love with others. Blessings, brothers and sisters.

–Jim and Jen

www.ingramcontent.com/pod-product-compliance
Lightning Source LLC
Chambersburg PA
CBHW010857090426
42737CB00020B/3407